A CLASSIC BIBLE CHAPTER

DANIEL 6
Surviving The Lions' Den

By

Allen C. Liles

DANIEL 6
Surviving The Lions' Den

by

Allen C. Liles
Liles Communications, LLC

Published By
Positive Imaging, LLC
bill@positive-imaging.com

ISBN: 9781951776633

This book is dedicated to my dear wife
and partner in ministry
Jan Carmen Liles

(1941-2017) RIP

Contents

INTRODUCTION

Buckle up for a great Bible story. It is full of faith in action, integrity, bravery, betrayal, and deliverance from dangerous plots. Chapter 6 of the Old Testament book of Daniel offers many blessings for believers. Faith in God's divine protection serves as perhaps the most important. Daniel was a revered palace administrator in Babylon when King Darius found himself manipulated into sending the prophet to certain death in a den of lions. The king valued Daniel's many talents. In fact, he was set to promote him over all the other kingdom officials. Daniel's rivals were jealous. They wanted him gone. A nefarious plan to depose the old prophet succeeded, mainly because Daniel had ignored the king's decree about worshipping anyone else but him. In his faithful mind, there was only one true God. That was the Deity he chose to worship. Since King Darius was obligated to punish any disobedience, Daniel was thrown to the lions. However, because of his steadfast faith in God, Daniel survived the roaring lions without a mark on him. The amazed king then directed his wrath at the plotters. They (along with their wives and families) were cast to the lions, where "their bones were crushed". Darius then ordered everyone to honor Daniel's God.

The story in Daniel 6 has considerable relevancy in today's world. Have you ever been thrust into your own den of lions? Has some outside force or individual ever plotted against you? Have you ever been terrified at the prospect of being mauled and destroyed? Did you experience feelings of abandonment and vulnerability? Perhaps you thought: "I will not survive" as the predators began gathering around you. In this crucial moment, where did you look for strength and courage? Did you ask God for deliverance? Or was the terror so strong that you were paralyzed with fear? Did you freeze, unable to take any meaningful action to save yourself? Perhaps you asked God for an angel to protect you, just like the one he sent Daniel.

We have all been thrown into the Lions' Den at some point in our human lives. Most of us survived, but perhaps still carry the scars of physical, emotional and spiritual attacks. Often our human journey can proceed for years without any major incident or upset. However, the nature of modern life almost assures that a den of lions awaits us. When that time comes, how will you handle it?

Without question, seeking God's divine assistance offers the best plan for survival. Placing our complete faith and trust in a higher power offers the surest plan for deliverance from harm. A loving God asks only for your call. Problems often grow larger when we delay getting our Creator involved. In Daniel's case, he had already shown his faithfulness to the one true God. He maintained a total belief that God would protect him from the lions.

What are the primary lessons we can learn from Daniel 6? Foremost is that we must trust God to deliver us from the challenges of daily life. When we remain faithful, God will stand up for us. The Lord bolsters our courage whenever danger threatens. God provides His whole armor (Ephesians 6: 10-18) when we encounter threats to our well-being. We are given many spiritual tools to defend ourselves, including a shield of faith and a breastplate of righteousness. In Daniel's case, God also dispatched a warrior angel to close the lion's mouths. On the next morning, after Daniel had been consigned to certain death, King Darius was relieved. He found his favorite prophet and administrator unmarked and intact. Then the king's wrath was turned on Daniel's enemies. They were unable to survive the Lion's attacks and were torn to shreds. Divine justice had prevailed, all thanks to Daniel's faithfulness.

No matter how threatening any "lions' den" may seem, maintaining a strong faith in God guarantees deliverance. If you are fearful of roaring lions in your own life, consider the story of Daniel. Read again how his unshakeable faith brought him through to victory over opposing forces. That can be the happy ending for your lions' den story as well.

Allen C. Liles

September, 2021

PREPARATION FOR STUDYING
DANIEL 6

OPENING PRAYER

"Dearest God and Creator of all life, help me find personal encouragement and support from the story of Daniel in the Lions' Den. Allow me to connect with the faith that he displayed without any fear of his own destruction. Let me use the powerful example of Daniel's trust to guide and direct my own responses. Whatever I may be facing, Daniel's unwavering commitment can provide divine guidance in my own challenges. Grant me peace and wisdom during these trying times. Thank you, God. Amen.

MEDITATION:

Locate a quiet place where you will not be disturbed or interrupted. Commit to sitting in the silence for a minimum of 15 minutes. Place both feet flat on the floor. Put both hands in your lap with the palms facing upward. Practice deep *breathing. Inhale five long breaths through your nose, counting from 1 to 5. After each breath, open your mouth and breathe out, again counting from 1 to 5. After completing the breathing exercise, read these words:*

"LORD, I need Daniel's faith, belief and courage. I find myself surrounded by roaring lions. They are threatening to destroy me. Please bless and understand my human need for reassurance and deliverance. Help me find the courage and bravery required to face any fear. If you are for me, who can be against me? I know that your power can save me from death and destruction. You are my divine protector. In the silence, I come to you now. Deliver me, God. Please tell me what I need to know."

Now sit quietly in the silence for a minimum of at least five minutes. Wait patiently for God's response. If you do not discern a reply from the Holy Spirit within you, do not worry. God can still answer your call for help at another time or place.

PRAYER OF THANKSGIVING

God, thank you for this peaceful time of communion with You. Please help me stay open and receptive to your wisdom and guidance. I especially need to find the faithfulness to survive the lions' den of my life. Stay by my side as shield and defender against the powers that seek to devour me. Send angelic protectors to close the mouths of those who want to harm me. Feel my total belief in your divine power against all negative forces. In your sacred Presence, I place my full trust. Thank you, thank you, thank you, God.

20 QUESTIONS ABOUT DANIEL 6

1 *Who was Daniel?*

Daniel was a major Old Testament prophet. He is believed to have authored the book of Daniel in the Holy Bible.

2 *When did he live?*

Approximately 605-530 BC

3 *What is the book of Daniel about?*

The entire book recounts the experiences of Daniel and his friends after they were taken hostage in Jerusalem by Babylonian King Nebuchadnezzar.

4 *How did Daniel get from Judah to Babylonia?*

Daniel was abducted from Jerusalem by King Nebuchadnezzar after he overran the city. The king ordered Ashpenaz, chief of his court officials, to bring the most talented captives to serve in the Babylonian royal palace. They would undergo three years of intense training before entering the king's service.

5 ***Who were Daniel's three famous friends also brought from Judah to Babylonia?***

The three young men were originally named Hananiah, Mishael, and Azariah. The chief official gave them new names: Shadrach, Meshach and Abednego, respectively. You know them from their survival of the fiery furnace. Daniel was also renamed Belteshazzar.

6 ***What was Daniel's claim to fame?***

Besides being one of God's major prophets, Daniel was an excellent administrator, gifted leader and unrivaled interpreter of royal dreams and visions.

7 ***Did Daniel author the Old Testament book that bears his name?***

Traditionally, yes.

8 ***Why did he write the book of Daniel?***

He wrote the book during Israel's captivity to foster and encourage a trust of God by the Jewish people.

9 ***How old was Daniel when he was thrown into the lions' den?***

Approximately 80 years of age.

10 ***Who threw Daniel to the lions?***

King Darius.

11 ***Why?***

Many of Daniel's contemporaries were jealous of his popularity and influence with King Darius. The officials (Satraps) plotted to get Daniel removed from the king's service. They convinced Darius to issue an edict that anyone caught worshipping any other God but him would be severely punished. Daniel ignored the decree and continued worshipping his God. His rivals informed the king of Daniel's blatant violation of the king's orders. They convinced the reluctant monarch to follow through on his threat of severe punishment. The Satraps were defined as the various palace officials, governors and different ethnic groups in each province.

12 ***Was King Darius reluctant to punish Daniel by throwing him to the lions?***

Yes. The king liked and valued Daniel. However, he was unable to find any legitimate way to avoid following through on his decree.

13 ***What happened?***

The worried king rushed to the lions' den the next morning to check on Daniel's safety. Darius found the prophet unhurt and intact. He was told that an angel from God had intervened and closed the lion's mouths.

14 ***How did King Darius react?***

He was overjoyed and relieved. He ordered that Daniel be lifted out of the lions' den. The king then sent Daniel's accusers, along with their wives and families, into the den. The lions overpowered everyone and "crushed their bones".

15 ***How did the King make amends to Daniel?***

Darius issued a new decree that everyone in his kingdom must fear and revere the God of Daniel.

16 ***What happened to Daniel after the incident in the Lions' Den?***

Daniel prospered until his death approximately five years later.

17 ***What were the biggest lessons presented in the book of Daniel?***

1. Devotion and faithfulness to God will be rewarded and

2. You shall worship no other Gods before the one true God.

18 ***Did Daniel display any fear of the Lions?***

The Bible does not mention any fear on Daniel's part.

19 ***Who was the angel that protected Daniel from the Lions?***

The angel is not named, but many believe it was Gabriel.

20 ***What does Daniel's name mean?***

The name Daniel comes from the Hebrew "For God is my judge".

DANIEL 6

BIBLICAL TEXT

NIV

(New International Version)

1. It pleased Darius to appoint 120 satraps to rule throughout the kingdom.

2. with three administrators over them, one of whom was Daniel. The satraps were made accountable to them so that the king might not suffer loss.

3. Now Daniel so distinguished himself among the administrators and satraps by his exceptional qualities that the king planned to set him over the whole kingdom.

4. At this, the administrators and satraps tried to find grounds for charges against Daniel in his conduct of government affairs, but they were unable to do so. They could find no corruption in him, because he was trustworthy and neither corrupt or negligent.

5. Finally these men said, “We will never find any basis for charges against this man Daniel unless it has something to do with the law of his God.”

6. So these administrators and satraps went as a group to the king and said, "May King Darius live forever!"

7. The royal administrators, prefects, satraps, advisors and governors have all agreed that the king should issue an edict and enforce the decree that anyone who prays to any god or human being during the next thirty days, except to you, Your Majesty, shall be thrown into the Lions' Den.

8. Now, Your Majesty, issue the decree and put it in writing so that it cannot be altered—in accordance with the law of the Medes and Persians, which cannot be repeated."

9. So King Darius put the decree in writing.

10. Now when Daniel learned that the decree had been published, he went home to his upstairs room where the windows opened toward Jerusalem. Three times a day he got down on his knees and prayed, giving thanks to his God, just as he had done before.

11. Then these men went as a group and found Daniel praying and asking God for help.

12. So they went to the king and spoke to him about his royal decree: "Did you not publish a decree that during the next thirty days anyone who prays to any other god or human being to you, Your Majesty, would be thrown into the lions' den?" The king answered, "The decree stands in accordance with the law of the Medes and Persians, which cannot be repealed."

13. Then they said to the king, "Daniel, who is one of the exiles from Judah, pays no attention to you, Your Majesty, or the decree you put in writing. He still prays three times a day."

14. When the king heard this, he was greatly distressed; he was determined to rescue Daniel and made every effort until sundown to save him.

15. Then the men went as a group to King Darius and said to him, "Remember, Your Majesty, that according to the law of the Medes and Persians no decree or edict that the king issues can be changed."

16. So the king gave the order and they brought Daniel and threw him into the lions' den. The king said to Daniel, "May your God, whom you serve continually, rescue you!"

17. A stone was brought and placed over the mouth of the den, and the king sealed it with his own signet ring and with the rings of his nobles, so that Daniel's situation might not be changed.

18. Then the king returned to his palace and spent the night without eating and without any entertainment being brought to him. And he could not sleep.

19. At the first light of dawn, the king got up and hurried to the lions' den.

20. When he came near the den, he called to Daniel in an anguished voice, "Daniel, servant of the living God, has your God, whom you serve continually, been able to rescue you from the lions?"

21. Daniel answered, "May the king live forever!

22. My God sent his angel and he shut the mouths of the lions. They have not hurt me, because I was found innocent in his sight. Nor have I done anything wrong before you, Your Majesty."

23. The king was overjoyed and gave orders to lift Daniel out of the den. And when Daniel was lifted from the den, no wound was found on him, because he had trusted in his God.

24. At the king's command, the men who had falsely accused Daniel, were brought in and thrown into the lions' den, along with their wives and children. And before they reached the floor of the den, the lions overpowered them and crushed all their bones.

25. Then King Darius wrote to all the nations and people's of every language in all the earth: "May you prosper greatly!"

26. "I issue a decree that in every part of my kingdom people must fear and reverence the God of Daniel. For he is the living God and he endures forever; his kingdom will not be destroyed, his dominion will never end.

27. He rescues and he saves, he performs signs and wonders in the heavens and on the earth. He has rescued Daniel from the power of the lions."

28. So Daniel prospered during the reign of Darius and the reign of Cyrus the Persian.

PRESENT DAY LIONS' DENS

"Lions' Dens" still exist today, if not literally. Many human beings must cope with feelings of being cast into daunting and dangerous circumstances. Here are some examples of today's lions' dens:

1. **ILL HEALTH**—Health challenges can occur without warning. Human beings have perfect health one day and find themselves bedridden the next. Many face the dread that comes with a bad medical diagnosis or sudden illness. When someone loses their health, it impacts everything else. Dealing with a serious illness requires faith, courage and determination.

2. **MONEY PROBLEMS**—For most people, having money issues can feel like being cast into a den of roaring creditors. Most human beings equate well-being with the size of their bank accounts. Not having enough money can produce fears of poverty. A lack of money often results in anxiety, depression and poor decisions.

3. **FAMILY ISSUES**—Separation, disagreements and estrangement from our human family can generate negative feelings. Abandonment issues, anger and resentments are

triggered. People often become distraught over family troubles. Not having strong family ties can resemble being left alone in a den of threatening lions.

4. **CAREER FAILURE**—Being unemployed or underemployed strikes at human self-esteem. It reduces self-worth and hinders one's ability to achieve personal satisfaction and fulfillment. Not having meaningful work can leave people vulnerable and searching for purpose.

5. **A LACK OF LOVING RELATIONSHIPS**—Being alone in the world's lions' den without one or more love relationships exposes us to feelings of deprivation and despair. We all need human connections. Nobody wants to face the lions of everyday life alone. Everybody needs someone to care about them.

6. **ADDICTIONS**—Various addictions represent the ultimate lions' den. Drugs, alcohol, sex, gambling, pornography and other common addictions can separate us from our spiritual moorings. The negative power of an addiction thrusts anyone into a dangerous and even life-threatening situation. Addictions possess the ability to "crush our bones" just like the threatening lions.

7. **AGING**—Many people are surprised how the aging process arrives almost unannounced. Of course, we expect that everyone will eventually get old. However, aging often sneaks up quietly when our attention is busy elsewhere. Becoming an "elderly" person in a fast-paced and technologically driven world brings numerous adjustments. Some of these challenges can feel as threatening as a den of roaring lions.

8. **MENTAL CONFUSION**—Dementia and Alzheimer's represent their own special nightmares. Losing one's mind, even in small increments, strips away a plethora of important tethers to human life. Being deprived of precious memories, personal relationships and a general quality of life can produce anger, anxiety, depression and hopelessness. The heartless lions who attack someone's fragile mind are especially cruel and uncaring.

9. **LEGAL PROBLEMS**—Coping with life in general can be daunting. But navigating the human scene while dealing with thorny legal issues can add another layer of discomfort. Most human beings are unaware of how getting caught up in the legal system can destroy their serenity and create financial challenges.

10. **SPIRITUAL CONCERNS**—When anyone is surrounded by snarling lions, trusting God becomes paramount. As with any threat to our well-being, holding on to our faith in God often becomes the only hope for survival. If a human being is struggling with his or her relationship with God, it can close off the best escape route from the hungry lions. Lacking a close bond with a Higher Power can render anybody defenseless. Maintaining a powerful faith becomes easier when we already possess a close personal relationship with our Creator.

THE SATRAPS PLOT AGAINST DANIEL

Satrap #1—"Listen up, you guys! I have some news that affects all of us. I have it on good authority that King Darius plans to appoint Daniel as the chief administrator over everybody."

Several Satraps in unison: "Oh no!"

Satrap #1—"Oh yes! You better believe it. This is not good news."

Satrap #2—"What can we do? Darius loves that Jerusalem Boy. In the king's eyes, old Danny can do no wrong."

Satrap #1—"It won't be easy. Daniel has no discernible faults. Look, I have examined the fool up one side and down the other. I cannot find anything wrong with him. The man is honest, smart and capable. I don't see any way to discredit him with the king."

Satrap #3—"Well, we must do something. We cannot have a "straight arrow" like Daniel watching our every move. He would make life miserable. We couldn't get away with anything."

Satrap #4—"We have always had problems with these guys from Jerusalem. Daniel and his three buddies are cut from the same cloth. You know who I am talking about."

Satrap #1—"Of course. You are referring to Mishael, Meshach and Abednego. They are just like Daniel. How did those guys ever survive the fiery furnace? That one is still a mystery to me. I don't like any of them. They are such stuck up hot shots."

Satrap #2—"Well, right now Daniel is the one we need to worry about. The other three are not as big of a threat. Maybe we can find another fiery furnace that works, if push comes to shove.

Several Satraps: "Hear, hear!"

Satrap # 3—"Does anyone have any ideas on how to deal with Daniel?"

Satrap #4—"I have one!"

Satraps #1 and #2-- "Well, let's hear it!"

Satrap #4—"Daniel is faithful about worshipping his precious God. If the king thought somebody was bowing down to anyone else but him, he would not like it. We all know about King D's ego."

Satrap #1—"We need to put some doubts in the king's feeble brain about Daniel. I like the idea of exploiting his faithfulness to his God. I don't know what else we can do."

Satrap #2—"How about suggesting that Darius put out a decree about "worship". It could state that anyone who bows down to any god but him would be cast into the lions' den. Knowing Danny's faithfulness to his God, I am sure he would flat-out ignore it. If we could then catch Daniel in the act, the king would have no choice. The lions' den would be the next stop. It would be the end for him."

Satrap #3—"I don't know. I have a feeling that Darius would try to wiggle out of punishing Daniel. He really loves the guy. We would have to paint the king into a corner where he is forced to go through with his decree."

Satrap #4—"The wording of the decree is key. If Darius publishes something very specific in writing, he would be too embarrassed to go back on it. Old Daniel's goose would be cooked."

Satrap #1—"I like it, I like it. It could be our only hope to stop Daniel before he comes into power over us. All in favor, say "Aye!"

All Satraps: "Aye!"

Satrap #1—"OK boys, let's get busy. The plot is on".

Satrap #2—"It sounds good to me. What do we have to lose? Time is a-wasting."

Satrap #3—"Do you think King Darius will suspect anything?"

Satrap #4—"Not a chance. Come on, boys. Let's get busy. This is the end for Mr. Dan. We won't have to worry about him anymore after the lions finish with him."

DANIEL DISCUSSES THE KING'S DECREE WITH GOD

DANIEL: "I'm sure you already know about the decree issued by King Darius about who and what his subjects are allowed to worship."

GOD: *"Of course."*

DANIEL: "I am surprised by it. Someone must have convinced him this was a good idea. I don't believe he could have thought this one up on his own."

GOD: *"You are right about that. The satraps are jealous of you. This is their plan to get rid of you."*

DANIEL: "How will they do it?"

GOD: *"They know you will never stop worshipping Me, no matter what Darius decrees. Not even a king could turn you away from Me. They plan to expose your defiance of the decree. Then Darius will have no other choice but to cast you into the lions' den."*

DANIEL: "I thought Darius was my friend."

GOD: *"He is. The king loves and appreciates you. That is why he chose you to rule over the satraps. It also represents the source of*

their jealousy. They hate your favor with the king. This plot is directed at removing you."

DANIEL: "What can I do about it?"

GOD: ***"At this point, your options are limited. The king signed the decree in public. Everybody knows about it. If he goes back on his word to punish any disobedience, it could create civil unrest. All monarchs have one main goal: preserving their power. Allowing you, or anybody, to defy him is not a good look for any royal."***

DANIEL: "I will not stop worshipping You, Father, under any circumstance. No royal decree will ever change that. So, what is my alternative?

GOD: ***"I can only think of one."***

DANIEL: "What is that?"

GOD: ***"You will have to trust that I can deliver you from the den of lions. Lift your faith to the highest level. You must believe in My divine Power to clamp shut the jaws of death."***

DANIEL: "You know that I trust you, My LORD. But that would be a miracle."

GOD: ***"Don't you know Me by now? Miracles are what I do!"***

DANIEL: "Yes, yes, I know. But the lions are formidable. No one has ever come out of their den alive."

GOD: ***"No one has ever trusted Me to deliver them before. Most human beings become paralyzed by fear when they see the lions. They forget all about Me. No one has ever thought to seek My protection before. Many just give up without asking for My help."***

DANIEL: "I can't think of anyone else who might be strong enough to protect me. How will you do it?"

GOD: ***Trust Me. I have the perfect angel for the job. I will send Gabriel. He will clamp shut the lions' jaws. They will be angry and paw about. However, they will be no match for Gabriel. He is a beast, but an angelic beast. The lions will be powerless against him."***

DANIEL: "What will happen after that? Won't King Darius be angry?"

GOD: ***"No. He king will be relieved. He did not want this to happen in the first place."***

DANIEL: "And the satraps?"

GOD: ***"When all is said and done, I would not want to be in their sandals! This is what happens when you plot against My servants. What goes around comes around."***

DANIEL: "Thank you for protecting me. I love you!"

GOD: ***"Right back at you, My beloved Son, in whom I AM well pleased."***

THE TWELVE GIFTS OF DANIEL 6

1. FAITH IN GOD
2. INTEGRITY
3. COMMITMENT
4. TRUST
5. STRENGTH
6. SURVIVAL
7. COURAGE
8. PERSEVERANCE
9. INTELLIGENCE
10. CONVICTION
11. BRAVERY
12. RESURRECTION

FAITH IN GOD

Whenever we maintain a strong faith in God, no lions' den can frighten us. Faith overcomes fear. It provides a steel cocoon that protects us from all dangers. Faith offers a sanctuary from anything that may threaten our well-being. When we remain faithful to God, our deliverance from all harm becomes assured. Faith acts as the backbone of our soul. It demonstrates God's ultimate promise to protect and defend us against all adversaries.

INTEGRITY

Daniel displayed great personal integrity in refusing to obey King Darius' decree. When we choose to act with honor, it reaffirms our dedication to spiritual principles. The material world often accepts corruption as a way of life. When someone refuses to go along with any form of dishonesty, negative forces become frustrated. Being in integrity requires the strength to stand against powerful voices. Evil seeks to present a lack of integrity as attractive and even "cool". Instead, failing to exhibit basic integrity can undo the most talented individual or well-meaning endeavor. You either have integrity or you do not. There is no such thing as partial integrity.

COMMITMENT

Daniel displayed an unyielding commitment to the one eternal God. It exceeded his devotion to King Darius. For Daniel, worshipping his God took precedence over anyone or anything on the material plane. Pledging his loyalty to God modeled an awareness of spiritual priorities. We should never fail to honor a commitment to God. As in the Lions' Den, our life could depend on it.

TRUST

Trust is synonymous with faith. Anyone standing before a roaring lion hopes for a spiritual miracle. Trusting in divine deliverance requires a higher level of belief. For many, hope of any kind often seems out of reach. Yet, as Daniel was being thrust into the lions' den, you can sense his confidence in the outcome. He had experienced God's Presence and Power many times before. Why would he doubt that the LORD would stand with him again as he faced the scary lions? Daniel trusted and believed in God's promise to never leave or forsake him.

STRENGTH

Of course, Daniel's diminished physical strength at his 80-plus years was no match for any lion. However, human strength was never the issue in this classic Bible story. Daniel possessed spiritual power of the highest order. With an angel sent by the LORD at his side, Daniel was able to survive. Although weak physically, his inner strength defied measurement. Daniel was supercharged both spiritually and mentally as he faced the roaring lions. Without question, the old prophet took more than an aging body into this challenge. Whatever your own circumstances, you can bring enhanced spiritual muscle into any dangerous situation. Asking for God's help brings divine power into the battle for survival.

SURVIVAL

Sometimes when we are trapped in a den of threatening lions, survival becomes our only goal. Human beings possess a "fight or flight" element in their DNA. Staring real or imagined death in the face can produce that response. Being locked in with the powerful lions eliminated Daniel's "flight" possibilities. He had no other option but to confront the beasts. God had already decided to send an angel who would close their mouths. There was no other escape plan. We always have the option of summoning God to protect us in times of imminent danger.

COURAGE

Daniel displayed personal courage throughout this famous Bible story. He defied the king's decree about who he could worship. The prophet did not try to hide his continuing devotion to God. Daniel was aware of the serious plot against him by the satraps. Yet, he refused to turn away from worshipping God. Throughout the Holy Bible, there are many examples of God's servants being silenced, beaten, imprisoned, persecuted, injured, killed and even crucified. What was a premier character trait that allowed them to remain faithful until the end? God endowed His spiritual followers with exceptional inner and outer courage during the most severe trials.

PERSEVERANCE

Perseverance is an important aspect of any successful spiritual life. God's Path can be steep and hard. Many people become discouraged and quit on the first difficult day. Only the most determined keep going when challenges arrive.. Without the willingness to persevere despite obstacles, following God's will can seem impossible. What produces a persevering attitude? The promise of a higher reward has kept many believers traveling on the Path to God's Kingdom. Without a persevering mind-set, the human brain might be convinced to fall away before reaching its sacred destination. Achieving our spiritual destiny requires an abundant supply of perseverance.

INTELLIGENCE

Daniel used his unique intelligence and wisdom to rise higher in position and influence . He also was aware of the consequences in going against King Darius' decree. However, the prophet showed that he trusted his own thinking—and God. He understood that the king had been hoodwinked by the satraps. Daniel was alert to their negative agenda. However, despite his knowledge of the situation facing him, Daniel stood strong against the plotters. His divine intelligence exceeded that of the enemies aligned against him. In the end, he walked unscathed out of the lions' den while his opponents were vanquished.

CONVICTION

Daniel's action demonstrated his unswerving belief in the power of God to save him. Nothing could intimidate or dissuade the prophet from worshipping his God. The world likes to test us. It wants to know the strength of our convictions. If a person is deemed weak, the jaws of evil can clamp down even harder. Daniel showed his deep convictions were unshakeable. His belief in God was sufficient to withstand any challenge. There was never one moment when Daniel wavered in his dedication to the Creator. His satrap opponents underestimated the prophet's unshakeable conviction. Daniel's devotion to God held firm, even when facing the frightening den of lions.

BRAVERY

Daniel probably did not regard his defiance of King Darius as brave. Yet, it was an example of bravery and courage to oppose a declared and signed decree. Flaunting the king's edict was exactly what the satraps wanted Daniel to do. The prophet did not disappoint. His decision to continue worshipping God set up a confrontation with the king. Daniel's foes deliberately placed him in jeopardy. Now, Darius was forced to deliver or be made to look weak. Being brave when the odds are against us takes inner nerve and a strong belief in the outcome. Having God on our side improves the odds in our favor.

RESURRECTION

Being thrown into any lions' den can feel like a crucifixion. Human beings often find themselves hoisted up on various crosses: financial problems, career failures, serious health issues, strained family relationships and battling addictions can all seem like crucifixion experiences. How are we to remain strong as these fearsome nails are pounded into our flesh? What miracle can save us from certain defeat? Our only hope in resurrection lies in maintaining our faith and trust in God. Spirit alone is the answer. Only His Power can clamp shut the jaws of lions and raise us up to live another day.

MORE ABOUT DANIEL

Daniel was one of God's best and most effective servants. He lived a productive and meaningful life of spiritual service. All four kings that Daniel served (Nebuchedezzar, Belshazzer, Darius and Cyrus) revered him. They recognized his unique executive and administrative skills. But the most appreciated contribution to the royal households was Daniel's God-given ability to interpret dreams and visions. Most Old Testament kings and queens, princes and princes were fixated on learning the real meaning of their nocturnal wanderings. Daniel's insight and wisdom in the art of dream interpretation fascinated the royalty he served. Many who occupy seats of power are often insecure in their status. They are fearful of being deposed or doomed to an grisly death. Their long-term status often appears tenuous to them. "Uneasy lies the head that wears the crown" from *King Henry, Part Two* was one of Shakespeare's most perceptive statements. Royalty can become obsessed with present and future events. It searches for hidden meanings and obscure clues in dreams and visions. Anyone in the king's court who possessed the gift of dream and vision interpretation received immediate favor. Daniel was without peer in this area. His inspired assessment of "the handwriting on the wall" for King Balshazzar secured Daniel's reputation. His prophetic insight earned him a coveted seat near the center of royal power. However, this multi-gifted man was more than just a "seer". Daniel was also a talented administrator. He excelled as an executive and manager, thus earning even more royal accolades. This, and the fact that he had originated from the royal household in Judah, made Daniel a danger to his peers. They were jealous of his proximity to power and his overall influence. Even worse for them, Daniel was honest. His incorruptible nature made him an absolute threat to the satraps and other officials. Therefore, they were constantly seeking to undermind him. The scheme to expose his violation of King Darius' decree seemed almost fool-proof. However, Daniel's foes underestimated the divine protection that God afforded one of His favorite prophets. Of course, a reluctant Darius was overjoyed when Daniel managed to survive the lions' den. He turned on the schemers and tossed them to the hungry lions. The plotters and their respective families were soon finished. Afterwards, Daniel received even more royal recognition and responsibility. Finally, there can be no greater honor than to have a storied book of God's Holy Word named specifically for you. The book of Daniel, resting between Ezekiel and Hosea attests to his important and unique place in Biblical history.

WHAT REALLY HAPPENED IN THE LION'S DEN

Several of the plotters against Daniel were present when the prophet was physically tossed into the lions' den. Seven hungry lions eagerly awaited his arrival. They had not been fed for several days. The schemers wanted no slip-ups. Daniel had enjoyed a privileged status in Babylonia ever since his abduction from the royal household in Jerusalem many years earlier. Now, Daniel's detractors wanted this interloper from Judah gone for good.

Daniel offered no resistance as he was escorted down into the lions' den. This puzzled the four satraps assigned to walk with him. The old man was even cordial, asking each their names. The satraps watched as Daniel ambled into the den, seemingly unconcerned. As the door shut behind him, the last thing the satraps saw was one of the lions slowly approaching an erect and upright man. His plotters were amazed at his bravery. Surely, he knew what was coming.

Here is the inside story of what transpired, out of everyone's view. The satraps had wanted to watch the spectacle of Daniel being eaten by the pride of Lions. However, as they cleared the den entrance, a huge form had suddenly confronted them. The “thing”, approaching ten feet in height, blocked their path. It carried a large tarpaulin. Without a word, the huge form threw the tarp over all four men. Then the “thing” administered a single blow to each of the four skulls. It was not hard enough to kill, just to render them unconscious. The gigantic intruder gently gathered the men to his bosom, carried them all to an adjacent room and secured the door.

Meanwhile, back in the den of lions, Daniel observed all seven of the beasts beginning to stir. One of the larger animals had already started approaching him. Daniel did not move. Instead, he looked upward and said, “God, please judge me worthy of your protection.” At that moment, the prophet became aware of an enormous presence standing by his side. It was a mammoth creature with broad wings and clad in a dazzling white robe. There was an air of authority swirling around its divine presence. Daniel immediately sensed that God had dispatched an angel from Heaven to protect him from the lions.

“Good evening, Daniel, “the angel said. “I am Gabriel. I was sent by God to guarantee your safety. In case I need backup, the Archangel Michael is guarding the door. He can be available at a moment’s notice. However, I doubt that we will require his services. The lions should be happy that I have drawn this assignment. I am gentler than Michael. I simply shut the jaws of any lion that dares come near you. He has been known to give their furry heads a hard twist. I do not expect we will need any extreme measures. I treat all animals with respect. However, I am also firm. The lions will quickly understand the reason for my presence in their den. They will also appreciate my strength. I do not anticipate any problems after the first encounters."

Just then, the lead lion roared and lunged at Gabriel. The angel deftly dodged the move and boxed the lion's right ear with a powerful force. The beast crouched down in surprise. It roared again, but in a somewhat less fearsome manner. The lion rose up, stalked toward the angel, and then lunged again. This time, Gabriel struck the animal hard with his fist right between the eyes. It staggered the lion, who soon retreated. Just then, another one of the beasts sidled forward and leaped up on its hind legs toward the angel. Gabriel came from the floor with a gloved hand and caught the flying lion under the chin. The animal did a complete somersault and landed on its back unconscious.

Daniel was suddenly aware of the other five lions milling about. They were exchanging questioning looks. Who are these strange humans? One of the lions laid down on his stomach and the others soon followed suit. They needed to ponder the situation before taking further action. Every few minutes or so, a lion would glance in Daniel's direction and emit a moderate roar. However, there were no more approaches for the time being.

Gabriel motioned for Daniel to walk with him to the opposite corner of the den. "They will let us alone for a while," the angel told the prophet. "However, right before dawn, they will make one final charge. I will ask Michael to join us before that happens. When the attack comes, we will place you between us. Do not worry. No lion will be allowed to touch you. It is imperative that King Darius finds you completely unmarked. God wants no misunderstanding about the totality of your protection. If you had a gash on your body, there might be a question about your safety. God wants to make a powerful impression on the king. After this event, the satraps will have no influence. In fact, King Darius will react by tossing your enemies to these hungry critters."

"Is there any chance I could convince God to spare them." Daniel asked.

"No," Gabriel replied, "The king is exercising his free will choice in punishing your enemies. They have earned a harsh reward."

"Thank you—and God-- for protecting me," Daniel said as he tapped the angel lightly on one of his large wings.

"It is our greatest pleasure," Gabriel replied, "You have earned it."

DANIEL'S THREE FRIENDS

When Babylonian King Nebuchadnezzar overwhelmed Judah and its King Jaholakim, he plundered more than natural resources and personal wealth. He also stripped the Jewish people of some of their best young people. Teenage Israelites with exceptional talent, looks and abilities were abducted and relocated to the king's court in Babylon. Those with the highest potential were placed into three-years of preparatory training. Among those chosen for extensive grooming were Daniel and his three friends Hananiah, Mishael and Azariah. The latter three would be renamed Shadrach for Hananiah, Meshach for Mishael and Abednego for Azariah. Daniel would also be given a new name: Belteshazzar. The four young recruits immediately displayed their proclivity to independent thinking. As part of their palace training, they were assigned to receive their food and drink from the king's table. But the relocated Israelites chose to not "defile" themselves with the unhealthy fatty menu. Instead, they asked for a diet of vegetables and water. Daniel even threw in a challenge to the king's official in charge of their training. He asked that the Jewish young men be provided their special fare for ten days. At the end of that time, they would be compared to the trainees receiving food and wine from the king's menu. When the challenge ended, Daniel and his friends appeared much healthier and better nourished than those eating the royal food.

At the end of their three-year preparation, the king interviewed Daniel and his three friends. After talking with the young men, he deemed them the best of the best. According to the first chapter of the book of Daniel, King Nebuchadnezzar found the young captives from Judah "ten times better than all the magicians and enchanters in the whole kingdom." (Daniel 1: 20). Daniel's three friends later were embroiled in a serious dispute with the king. He had built a huge golden idol and ordered that everyone bow down before it. Anyone who failed to comply would be thrust into a "blazing furnace". (Daniel 3: 4-8) When it was reported that Daniel's three friends had disobeyed the king's decree, some astrologers in the royal court demanded they be thrown into the fiery furnace. The angry king sent for Shadrach, Meshach and Abednego. He demanded that they explain their disobedience. They replied: "King Nebuchadnezzar, we do not need to defend ourselves before you in this matter. But if we are thrown into the blazing furnace, the God we serve is able to defend us from it and he will deliver us from your majesty's hand. But even if he does not, we want you to know, your Majesty, that we will not serve your gods or worship the image of gold you have set up." (Daniel 3: 16-18). Their response infuriated King Neb. He ordered the blazing furnace turned up seven times hotter than normal. He then ordered some of his strongest soldiers to tie up the three and throw them into the fire. In fact, the flames proved so hot that many of the soldiers died as they drew near the heat. Shadrach, Meshach and Abednego were bound and thrown fully clothed into the furnace. King Nebuchadnezzar himself gazed into the fire and exclaimed "I see four men walking around in the furnace unbound and unharmed, and the fourth looks like the son of the gods." (Daniel 3:25). At that point, the king shouted for the three Jewish men to come out of the fiery furnace. The satraps, perfects, governors and royal advisors crowded around them. They were amazed that the flames had not scarred any of the three young men. The King shouted "Praise be the god of Shadrach, Meshach and Abednego, who has sent an angel and rescued his servants! They trusted in him and defied the king's command and were willing to give up their lives rather than serve and worship any god except their own God. Therefore, I decree that the people of any nation who say anything against their God be cut into pieces and their houses turned into piles of rubble, for no other God can save in this way." (Daniel 3: 26-28) Then the king promoted Shadrach, Meshach and Abednego and put them in total charge of the province of Babylonia.

The miracles of both the fiery furnace and the lions' den impacted the kings involved and the other Babylonian officials. For the satraps and their peers, it gave them yet more reason to distrust the four "golden boys" from Judah. But no one could deny that their powerful God and His angels had spared them all from terrible deaths. The two miracles also made deep impressions on the royal households that the four men served. The God of Daniel, Shadrach, Meshach and Abednego had proven Its awesome power. Many of the plotters died painful deaths. It was a warning best heeded by anyone planning to scheme against the four captives from Jerusalem.

DANIEL: THE DREAMS AND VISION GUY

Daniel is probably best known for his close encounter with the lions in their den. However, his lasting claim to biblical fame rests as an interpreter of dreams and visions for the four kings of Babylon whom he served. Kings Nebuchadnezzar, Belshazzar, Darius the Mede and Cyrus the Persian all valued Daniel's vast interpretative skills. Only Belshazzar's father King Nabonidus, who served just briefly before going into exile, did not utilize Daniel's ability to interpret dreams and visions. The prophet's overall reputation was bolstered, not only from his visionary gifts, but also by Daniel's honesty, uncompromising steadfastness, and unique administrative skills. Most good rulers value honest feedback based on rigorous honesty. The ones who only seek admiration and obedience rarely last. However, there is a natural tendency for advisors and officials not to criticize their leaders or bring them bad news. A lack of candor by those surrounding power often dooms any organization, nation or kingdom. Into this failure by Babylonian officials to level with their respective kings, Daniel stepped unafraid. He provided devastating clarity and fearless perspective. His interpretations came from a spiritual insight impossible to duplicate. The Holy Spirit provided the prophet's wisdom and knowledge. Daniel's also earned a stellar reputation in administrative areas, modeling exceptional leadership talents. That helped him to maintain continuing credibility with his various kings.

During his period of service to the various courts, Daniel interpreted several major dreams and visions. Perhaps the most familiar is "The Handwriting on the Wall" as told in the 5th chapter of Daniel. Belshazzar, son of King Nabonidus, had become the effective ruler of the Babylonian Empire while his father was in exile. Belshazzar threw an extravagant feast for the royal court, primarily to buck up the spirits of his depressed subjects. Times were rocky. There had been economic setbacks. A severe famine was impacting the kingdom and creating an atmosphere of negativity. Belshazzar answer to these troubles was to throw a party. He invited 1000 of his nobles and ordered that the gold and silver goblets taken from the temple in Jerusalem be used at the dinner. During the great feast, a hand suddenly appeared and began writing a strange message on the wall of the palace. In Aramaic, the words read: ***"Meme, meme, tekel, upharsin".*** The king watched the hand as it wrote. His face turned pale. He was so frightened that his legs grew weaker and his knees began knocking. The king summoned his "enchanters, astrologers and diviners" to interpret the strange writing, but they did not have a clue as to the meaning. Belshazzar became more terrified. His face grew even paler. At that point, the Queen entered the banquet hall. She reminded Belshazzar that King Nebuchadnezzar had appointed the prophet Daniel as the chief interpreter of dreams and visions. She urged the king to summon the old man to come and decipher the writing on the wall. Daniel was brought before the king, who promised to place a gold chain around his neck and make him the third highest ruler in Babylon if he could successfully interpret the handwriting. Daniel begged off from any rewards or honors. But he did interpret the message and it was not good news for Belshazzar. He noted that Nebuchadnezzar's prideful attitude and lack of humility had eventually resulted in his removal as king. Daniel castigated Belshazzar for his own lack of humility and failure to learn anything from King Neb's disgraceful exit. He accused the king of setting himself up in opposition to the one true God. Daniel even referred to using the golden goblets from the Temple in Jerusalem as evidence of Belshazzar's arrogance. Daniel then told the king that God had sent the hand to inscribe the message on the wall. He interpreted the writing as saying: "God has numbered the days of your reign and brought it to an end. You have been weighed on the scales and found wanting. Your Kingdom is divided and given to the Medes and Persians." That very night, according to Daniel 5, Belshazzar was killed and Darius the Mede took over the Kingdom. Daniel's proficiency in interpreting "the handwriting on the wall" restored him to a place of prominence in the new regime. At the time, the prophet was more than 80 years old. At the end of his days, Daniel could take great pride in a lifetime of service to God and his four kings.

MODERN DAY STORIES OF PEOPLE IN THE LIONS' DEN

TAHESHA

Tahesha Mae Johnson, 19, had misplaced her cell phone. She searched throughout her parent's tidy house on Emerald Avenue near downtown Chicago. No luck. It was now becoming a definite crisis. She needed to confirm hookup times for tonight with her three best friends. Now, she had no phone. Without an ability to text or call, Taisha was helpless. She was now into the desperate stage of digging through the house. As a distant but not likely possibility, Tahesha strode into her brother Anthony's bedroom. The 17-year-old was out somewhere, probably up to no good. Her phone was not in obvious sight, but Tahesha decided to dig through the bureau where "A" kept his tee shirts and underwear. Underneath the top layer of clothes, Taisha's outstretched hand touched two unexpected objects. She first pulled out a one-gallon storage bag stuffed with weed. This find was not surprising. She knew Anthony had a big-time love affair with pot, especially the potent new stuff with supercharged THC. The second item was more troublesome. It was a small caliber handgun. Taisha knew it as a "Saturday Night Special", a common weapon on the dangerous streets of Chicago. At least two of her girlfriends carried stylized versions of the small gun in their purses. Well, at least her brother's pistol was still in the bureau drawer. So, although Anthony may be out patrolling the streets, at least he was not carrying. She wondered if her brother had joined a gang yet. Tahesha's parents were terrified that Anthony, who was a decent athlete and somewhat straight arrow, might choose to check out the gangster life. Everybody in the family knew someone that had been murdered. Life on the crazy streets of Chicago was now problematic and downright dangerous. Just then, the telephone in the kitchen began ringing. Both of Tahesha's parents were at church tonight. They never missed the Wednesday night prayer meeting. She scurried down the stairs to answer the ringing. She had urged her folks to ditch their land line, but they were hopelessly old fashioned.

Tahesha picked up and heard her brother's frightened voice.

"Hesh, is Pops there?" Anthony asked. She could tell he was scared. His voice was quivering.

"What's wrong, "A"? Tahesha inquired, "Where you at?"

"I need Pops to come quick and bring some cash," Anthony said. "I need $500 right now or these dudes are going kill me."

"Now, listen to me, little bro," Tahesha said in a stern voice, "Mom and Pop ain't here. They both gone to Prayer Meeting at church. And even if they were here, they don't have $500 lying around the house to bail you out. What is going down? What kind of trouble you in? I know you do not have your peashooter on you because I just found it in your room. Who got you? What have you gone and done?"

"The "Lions" got me, 'Hesh," Anthony said in a low voice. "I've heard about them. They are a new street gang from Mexico City. All of them are ex Cartelers. They came cross the border in South Texas last week. They out to make a name for themselves up here. They been yanking people off the street and making them cough up either cash or drugs. I did not have my weed stash on me, so they want some paper instead. Say, if you have been snooping through my drawer, maybe you could bring the weed over to me? They might take the pot and let me slide. It's primo dope. It loaded with THC. Hurry! One of these Lion guys got a AK-47. He has been tickling the back of my neck with it and telling me how many brothers he offed back in Mexico. I don't think he be playing with me."

"Where exactly you at?" Tahesha asked.

"I'm in the back of a green van parked across the street from our house", Anthony answered. "I had just stuck my head out our house when these bros snatched me. Go out on the porch and look outside. You can see me."

Tahesha carefully placed the phone on the kitchen counter and opened the front door. She peered out and saw a dark green van with its parking lights on.

She went back to the kitchen and picked up the phone.

"How many of them got you," she asked,

"Four "Lions" are in the van with me and a couple more are on look-out," Anthony whispered, "Don't even think of calling Chicago PD. I would be dead before they could get here."

Suddenly, Tahesha heard an angry shout. "Hey homey! Somebody better be coming with the money or you dead," a loud voice yelled.

She could hear Anthony say: "Hey man, my folks are at church. But I have drugs. I promise it be great weed. The THC will blow your minds. I told my big sister to bring it over here. Just give us a minute, will you?"

"A minute is all you got now, bro. Your dumb sister better be walking in here right now, or we'll split your thick skull and then shoot you in the butt for good measure. We tired of messing with your m-----r f------g black ass. Now muy pronto, man! Su que tarde!"

"Hurry up Tash," her brother begged. "Get my dope and run it over here now! These crazy guys mean f----g business."

Tahesha hung up the phone, raced upstairs and grabbed the baggie of weed. She also scooped up the pistol and slipped it into the back pocket of her blue jeans. She was not about to let these Mexican gangsters hurt her brother.

Before she walked out the door, Tahesha decided to try and notify her folks at church. She knew her mother carried a cell phone with her everywhere now.

Mrs. Johnson picked up immediately.

"What's wrong?" her mother asked in a low voice. Alice Johnson knew Tahesha would never bother her at church unless there was a real problem.

"Anthony has gotten himself kidnapped in front of our house," Tahesha explained quickly. "They are some ex-cartel dudes from Mexico. It's a new gang in town called "The Lions".

"What are they doing in Chicago?" Mrs. Johnson inquired, as if that might make some a difference.

Then, Tahesha heard her father's voice from a distance, asking what the call was about.

"Anthony got himself grabbed by some bad people," Mrs. Johnson told him, "It's a gang named "The Lions".

"I've got to go," Tahesha said, "If I don't bring them what they want, Anthony could get shot."

"Pops and I will pray that our son gets away from these so-called Lions'," Mrs. Johnson said calmly, "If God can deliver Daniel from a den of lions, He can save Anthony."

For a second, Tahesha had trouble understanding what her mother was talking about. Then she understood. But this was not some Sunday School Bible story. These cartel gangsters were real and meant business.

Tahesha checked the baggie of marijuana and the Saturday Night Special tucked in her back pocket. As she hurried out the door, she came upon an enormous black form standing on the sidewalk in front of her house. He was the biggest thing she had ever seen.

As she approached the large presence, she thought "This dude is tall—and he's big too. He is more than NBA tall. Who is he?"

Without a word, the figure stepped up and snatched the baggie of marijuana from Tahesha. He tossed it into the bushes in front of the house.

"What the hell?" She cried out in surprise.

"I'll take the pistol too," he said, "Hand it over now!"

Tahesha was too stunned not to comply. She handed the gun over and watched as he bent its barrel backward with his bare hands.

"Now, come along with me," the figure ordered.

They both strode briskly towards the van, with Tahesha almost unable to keep up. The tall presence seemed to take his steps in leaps and bounds.

Just then, two smaller forms jumped out of the darkness.

"You must be the look-outs," Tahesha's companion said. "Well, you better look out." With that, he grabbed them both by their shoulders and violently banged their heads together. They both collapsed without a whimper.

When they reached the van, the enormous "thing" grabbed the back door of the vehicle and ripped it open with one quick motion.

"What the hell?" came a surprised voice. Tahesha peered inside and saw four figures surrounding her brother. They were all garbed in deep brown leather jackets and matching leather pants. All of them had long dark hair that curled around their faces. She thought they resembled human versions of miniature lion-like creatures.

"This is crazy!" she thought.

One of the ex-cartel members shouldered his AK-47 automatic weapon. He raised it up to shoot at the large figure and Tahesha. However, before the man could begin firing, the huge presence grabbed the barrel of the gun and ripped it out of the surprised man's hands. Then, he proceeded to use the weapon like a scythe. He struck every gang member hard across their knees. All four dropped into a common pile and began screaming in real pain.

"You hurt us," one of the men said, "Who are you?"

"I'm somebody you never want to see again," the large black form answered. "When we leave, I want you to get out on the freeway and start driving. Do not stop until you get to

Del Rio, Texas. Cross over the border at Piedras Negras and then disappear back into Mexico. If I ever see any of you in the U. S again, I will tear off each of your heads like chickens. Do I make myself clear, amigos?"

Then the enormous form gathered Anthony and Lakesha up under his wing-like arms and swept them out of the van. He carried the pair back to the Johnson's front porch.

"Before I go, Anthony," the figure said, "Let me say something, bro. I want you to lose the super weed and the pea shooter. Neither one is any good for you, little man. Dig? You got a good future if you clean things up. You might even be starting in the NFL someday. Now, both of you, go back inside and call your mother, Let Mrs. Johnson and Pops know that we got their 911 call. Tell them that everything is A (for Angel) OK. No need to worry."

Across the street, the green van cranked up and sped away. These four "Lions" were never seen again on the streets of Chicago.

JOHN AND LORETTA

John and Loretta Young were both raised as high achievers by their upper middle class Texas parents. Loretta's League City mom and dad had both worked for NASA in the early high-flying days of the space program.

Her mother Joan was a secretary in Shorty Powers' public affairs office. Loretta's father Raymond Franklin was in the room when Jim Lovell called out "Houston, we have a problem" during the nail-biting Apollo 13 mission. Meanwhile, John's parents were medical people in Houston. They were contemporaries of the famous surgeons Michael DeBakey and Denton Cooley and knew them both (DeBakey was clearly a genius but they both liked Cooley better). His dad, Dr. John Young, Sr, was head of the Ear, Nose and Throat department at St. Luke's Hospital. He had married Angela, the ENT department's nursing supervisor, in the late 1960s. John had arrived in 1970. Loretta was an only child as well. She had been named for the famous film and TV star Loretta Young. Her parents could never have anticipated their striking dark-haired daughter would someday end up marrying a man with the last name of Young. Now, the couple could claim a full-fledged Loretta Young as a daughter. John and Loretta had never met growing up in the Houston area. The NASA crowd and the medical community were both insular. The couple did not come into contact until a Greek mixer at the University of Texas in their junior year. John was a member of Kappa Sigma and Loretta was a Zeta Tau Alpha. They both lived in their respective fraternity and sorority houses. The pair clicked immediately. Both were business majors and discovered they had taken several classes together. Each planned on a corporate career as the surest path to wealth and status. Sex had also become important to both and, in that mystery, they also proved compatible. Within four weeks of their first meeting, the couple split for a long and loving weekend at the Monteleone Hotel in New Orleans. They became engaged after two Hurricanes apiece at Pat O'Brien's in the French Quarter. John recalled staggering back to the hotel and trying to go through the revolving front door on his hands and knees. They had taken their vows less than a year later, one week after graduation. The newly married couple stuck around Austin long enough to rack up a master's degree apiece in Business Management. John then signed on with Exxon as a fast-track executive trainee in Houston, while Loretta landed a job with a fledgling energy company in town with the curious name of Enron. They bought a condo in River Oaks and set about claiming their fame and fortune. The future looked gold-plated. They had decided to forego children until their career paths were established. So, they asked themselves, what could possibly go wrong?

It was not that John and Loretta had grown up with trouble free lives. After the Apollo missions in the 70s, the glory of space exploration began to fade. The Carter administration years were disastrous for the adrenalin junkies among the Johnson Space Center alumni. Although Joan's PA group were harder drinkers in the beginning, the sober-minded scientists soon caught up. Loretta's dad Raymond got roaring drunk for the first time at his 30th birthday party. Over the next three years, he accumulated two DUIs, a suspended Texas driver's license and a termination notice from a U. S. government contractor. Loretta spent most of her middle and high school years trying to counsel both parents. Mother Joan became a blackout drinker. Many nights she strolled out into their front yard wearing only her bra and panties. The traffic jams were sometimes backed up for two blocks. She and the League City police chief still exchanged Christmas cards. Raymond Franklin had finally salvaged his career somewhat. He latched onto a mid-level job at Halliburton through a Mission Control golfing buddy. Meanwhile, John's medical parents were confronting their own demons. His mother Angela became a pill head with blinding speed. She was on a first name basis with every pharmaceutical rep that called on the ENT group. She always claimed first dibs on the exotic new drugs far removed from Prozac Nation. Angela soon turned husband John on to the Magical Mystery world of big-time mind-altering drugs.

Trying to surgically remove someone's tonsils while navigating a colorful trip on LSD proved to be Doctor John's undoing. After a few years, the once respected doc was unable to secure any malpractice insurance. He soon left St. Luke's for the VA. Dr. Young had found that diminished gig through a friendly financial consultant with ties to Dr. Cooley. John had been forced to complete a stint in drug rehab first, a requirement that Loretta's mom Joan's front yard underwear escapades also had produced for her. The bottom line: each set of loving parents had provided a lions' den of addiction platforms for both John and Loretta, long before their first meeting and subsequent marriage.

Not that John and Loretta had grown up unaware of their respective family dysfunction. John's grandfather on his dad's side was also a Houston area physician who had died of alcoholism in his 50s. Loretta's grandmother on her mom's side was a raging drunk who had been in and out of mental institutions for years. She had received more than one "shock treatment" to rectify her mental deficiencies. "Nana" finally passed in her 80s in a nursing home for people with alcohol induced brain trauma. Both John and Loretta had been in and out of Alateen meetings when they were growing up. Witnessing alcohol and drug addiction first-hand had kept John and Loretta on a somewhat sober path, at least through high school. The only one of their parents who had ever sought and embraced recovery was Raymond Franklin. Loretta's father was a well-known presence at AA meetings in the upper Gulf Coast. Many of his hard-drinking NASA buddies had already found AA when Raymond first joined the fellowship in 1980. That included a few ex-astronauts, and one who had walked on the moon. However, Loretta's mother Joan had never once darkened the door of AA, except for required meetings while stuck in rehab. Joan had vowed to keep the family secrets to the grave. On John's side, his mother Angela had tried NA (Narcotics Anonymous) for a few exploratory meetings. However, the 12-step concept just never clicked in her pill-indoctrinated brain. Now in her 70s, she still looked forward to her daily regimen of the latest medications. Angela's personal physician ("Dr. Prescription Pad") was a more than willing participant in her addiction. Although Oxy had never interested her, Tramadol had definitely become the love of her life. Angela floated through a quiet and almost comatose life, only half aware of the world around her. Increasingly, she wanted it that way.

John and Loretta put the family addictions aside as they had both loped off to the University in Austin. Both loved the sprawling and friendly school and everything about it. They pursued Greek affiliations during their sophomore years, without a thought to the well-deserved reputation for rampant drinking at fraternity and sorority mixers. Kappa Sig had just completed a probationary period for alcohol abuse the year before John pledged. Zeta had been reprimanded several times over the years for various sisters lying passed out in the flower beds around the House. At first, neither John nor Loretta had been more than moderate drinkers. However, he soon developed a taste for Grant's 8 scotch. It became his highly regarded drug of choice. Loretta, strangely enough, settled on beer as her favorite. She loved Coors Lite and, of course, Lone Star. She would buy a six-pack of both around noon on Friday at a 7-Eleven on The Drag and then nurse them though the weekend. Neither John nor Loretta considered alcohol even a remote problem. Their career paths in the business school were far more important. Nor did they think much about their respective families' addiction problems, despite strong evidence to the contrary. Neither saw alcohol or prescription drugs as resembling anything like a den of lions just waiting to devour them.

John and Loretta's corporate paths did take some interesting turns. As an executive trainee for Exxon, John's program included some long stretches away from Houston. He was assigned to a drilling rig site between Midland and Odessa for an extended period. He loved the good old boys from West Texas. They were a high spirited, hard drinking bunch of oil field vets. John, (labeled "The Preppie") was accepted right away into the rowdy bar-hopping and all-night card playing. More than a few of the oil patch boys shared his love of Grant's 8. It produced an unexpected and beloved bond. John looked forward to the camaraderie. Meanwhile, Loretta adored her corporate gig with the hot shot Enron crowd. They were the hippest bunch in Houston, or at least that is what they told themselves and anyone who would listen. Loretta knew "high-flyers" when she saw them. After all, she was raised around the original NASA rocketeers. Enron was headed for the stock market stratosphere. Loretta was happy to go along for the ride. The drinking and partying aspect were a bit too rich for her taste, so she just nibbled at the fringes. Loretta soon caught the eye of an Enron whiz kid who had recently separated from his wife. She saw the executive's original flirtations as harmless. but with John gone so much, they spiced up her life. When the Enron ace drunkenly tried to kiss her at an office party, Loretta was able to rebuff him without consequences. However, the heady culture and John's absences finally took their toll. One day, the exec had suggested an afternoon tryst at a nearby company condo. It had been Loretta's only indiscretion, but it worried her. She had enjoyed it. The situation became moot when the Enron exec and his wife reconciled. He and Loretta were never alone together again.

Life proceeded for a time on autopilot. Then, a couple of unexpected events disrupted the status quo, On the eve of their fourth wedding anniversary, Loretta discovered she was pregnant. She found herself worried that John might not be the father. What a can of worms that would be! John seemed happy about the pregnancy, so the couple prepared for the birth of their first child. The ultrasound confirmed it was a girl. They decided to name the new baby Angela Joan Young, after their respective mothers. Loretta immediately put her beer drinking on hold. She had never really smoked cigarettes or done weed, but they were both canceled as well. John saw no reason to curtail his scotch drinking, but he did negotiate less time away from Houston. The second thing that happened was that John, Sr. lost his license to practice medicine. The VA had been patient with Dr. Young, but his alcoholism was creating problems. The state board pulled all medical privileges after he crashed his car into some customers at an outdoor restaurant. Nobody died, but it represented the capper to a faltering professional career. As part of the legal proceedings, the former doctor was sentenced to spend six full months at a Beaumont treatment center. All told, it was a personal and financial catastrophe. Yet that was not everything that befell the family. Years before, when he was at St. Luke's, John Sr. had invested in one of Denton Cooley's real estate ventures. The ill-considered and expensive project had caused the legendary heart doc to declare bankruptcy. John Young also lost a small fortune, as did many other doctor investors. The downward trajectory for the family was accelerating. John Sr. and wife Angela had already downsized from a River Oaks mansion to a small condominium off Westheimer Road. Now either Chapter 7 or Chapter 11 bankruptcy loomed for them as well.

Still, the "Lions' Den" of family addiction and dysfunction eluded both John, Loretta and their parents (except for her dad). Raymond Franklin had been trying to sell the recovery benefits of AA to both families for years. However, no one was interested. Nor did Narcotics Anonymous or support groups like Al-Anon create any desire for more information. John and Loretta's Alateen days had long since been forgotten. Then, one night in West Texas, when John was sleeping off a raucous night of partying with the roughneck crowd, he had a strange and terrifying dream. In the dream, he was alone in a darkened pit. Suddenly, he heard the roar of lions only a few feet away. He strained hard to check out the beasts. He counted seven of the frightening monsters. Each was wearing a golden crown with identifiable writing. He could barely make out the stenciled lettering. A crown on one of the lions' heads read "ALCOHOL""; another proclaimed "DRUGS"; "SEX" was written on the third lion's crown and "MONEY" on yet another of the beasts. The other three lions wore crowns that read "CODEPENDENCY", "DENIAL" and "EGO", respectively. In his terrifying dream, John saw the lions start to move in his direction. They were snarling and showing their teeth. Suddenly, he heard the blare of trumpets. He wondered if still more lions were being announced. The door leading into the pit was thrown wide open. Seven enormous white robed figures paraded into the pit and took positions by his side. They each wore a sash across their robe, with bright blue lettering. John surveyed them one by one. There was "SOBRIETY", "HONESTY", "FIDELITY", "COURAGE", "STRENGTH", "HUMILITY" and "VIRTUE". With a quick motion, each huge form took up a position opposite a lion. Then, with a swift and powerful action, they all reached out and closed the mouths of every roaring lion. It was suddenly silent in the den of lions. John yelled out "Thank you, thank you, thank you God!" Next to him in bed, Loretta awoke and asked: "What the hell is going on, John?". She asked. "Did you have a bad dream?" He thought for a few seconds and then answered. "No, I think it may have been a good one."

The following Saturday night, a full row at Raymond Franklin's AA homegroup meeting was taken up by Franklin and Young family members. They were all there, each wearing a distinctive white shirt or blouse. Everyone had their shirt sleeves rolled up to the elbow. It was time for the two families to come together in recovery. A new daughter and granddaughter would be arriving soon. The roaring lions of family addictions needed addressing now.

AUNT HARRIETT

Old Aunt Hariett had just turned 95. She was sickly and bedridden. However, the ancient woman still had no intention of dying. She was now becoming a legitimate problem for the devoted hospice team members that cared for her 24/7. Harriet had outstayed the maximum time allowed for hospice patients by a full three months. More than a few terminally ill people arrived in hospice and passed within one day. A quick exit was not for stubborn

Aunt Harriet. If anything, the determined old lady was clinging to life more now than when she first arrived in hospice nine months ago.

Her devoted family members tried everything to convince Harriett to let go. They brought in a chaplain from the hospice staff who talked with her about the glories of Heaven. The church going members of Harriett's large family brought priests, rectors and ministers to her bedside. All spoke in great depth about God's golden cycle of life and death. Harriet did not debate or disagree with any religious viewpoint. She would just flash her somewhat twisted "Right, right" smile and then ring the duty nurse for an early shot of medication. After a while, the pastoral visits stopped. The family did convene one official meeting about Harriett, but no solution emerged. More than one family member expressed a hope that God might somehow intervene on their behalf.

Aunt Harriett was well-to-do, so that compounded the lack of family patience. Only her long-time attorney (or "Mr. Grumpy" as the family called him) knew anything about her finances. He was not forthcoming with any information, except to say that he was henceforth serving as executor of her estate "pro bono". That was puzzling to some family members. They had long ago decided that

"Grumpy" had ulterior motives regarding Harriett's money. The "pro bono" thing made them wonder. What was in it for him now?

One early evening, the hospice's longtime maintenance man "George" was mopping the floor of her room. The elderly black gentleman was in his mid-70s but still needed to work. He always wore a starched white shirt with a bow tie. Word around the hospice unit was that "George" had been a pastor or lay leader at a black church before being forced to retire. He and Aunt Harriet had occasionally spoken but never chatted for more than a few seconds.

As George navigated near her bed, the old lady raised a wrinkled hand to get his attention. The sudden move caused him to backpedal.

"Wait a minute there, George," she said in a surprisingly strong voice, "I need to talk with you."

"Yes, mam," he stammered. Her unusual behavior seemed to confuse him.

"Please come over here and sit with me for a minute," Harriet said, "I won't bite."

George looked down at his mop and pail, and then carefully placed them adjacent to the front door. After making sure the door was fully open, he pulled up a chair near Harriet's bed.

"I want to ask you a question," Harriet said, "I want you to be honest with me."

"I will sure try, ma'm," George responded.

"Good," she nodded, "How much money do you have on you."

George looked startled again.

"You mean right now, in my pants pocket?"

"Yes, and in your billfold too. Be sure and count everything. I need a grand total."

The maintenance man wondered if the old lady wanted him to fetch something for her from the vending machine.

"Come on now, chop-chop," Harriet grinned. George had never seen her smile before.

He reached inside his right front pants pocket and found a few loose coins.

"Count it!" she almost demanded.

George looked in his hand. There were six quarters, two dimes and a nickel.

"I've got exactly two dollars," he told her.

"What about in your billfold?" Harriet asked.

George reached in his back pocket and extracted an old worn billfold. He felt almost embarrassed by its appearance.

"Well. let me see," he said, peering inside.

"I've got five singles," he stated. "I guess that makes it seven dollars in all. Not too flush right now, I'm afraid. Social Security don't hit until next Wednesday."

"Well, sir, I have some news for you," Harriet smiled. "You have exactly six dollars and three cents more than I do. My lawyer was here today. He told me that I have ninety-seven cents left in my checking account."

"Really, ma'm? I don't believe that for a second," George said, shaking his head.

"Yes, it was true before he came to tell me that some unexpected money arrived yesterday. An old stock that I owned 10 years ago finally settled with its shareholders. He brought me a check for ten thousand dollars. Do you want to see it?

Before waiting for his response, Harriet reached under her pillow. She produced the check and held it up in front of her so George could read it.

The maintenance man squinted at the check.

"It do say $10,000" he agreed, "Is it for real?"

"Yes," Harriet replied, "But it's a problem for me. You see, George, I had four million dollars in my account when I came into hospice. But I gave every nickel of it away the first day. I told my attorney to cut four checks for one million each. I gave the money to the Cancer Society, the Heart Association, the college I attended and the Girl Scouts. I was a Girl Scout once, back when I was growing up."

"That's right generous, ma'm," George said.

"I was pleased to do it," Harriett smiled, "However, I did not tell my family. They would be so upset with me. Whenever they come around here now, I feel like I'm in a lions' den. They are always pawing around my room, deciding who will have me for lunch first."

The maintenance man just shook his head.

"Money do some mighty strange things to people," he finally allowed.

"Now, I'm too embarrassed to die," Harriet said. "I feel guilty about disinheriting them all. I do not want these people saying bad things about me, although they never paid much attention to me before. I just cannot stand the thought of them fighting over my estate after I am gone."

George looked puzzled. "Well, I don't see that as no reason not to die," he said. "Don't you get tired of living sometime? I sure do. I also don't see Heaven as a bad place. Ain't no hungry lions pawing around looking for your cash up there."

"Absolutely," the woman said, "But I don't know how I can die and let them find out I was penniless."

"Wait a minute," George reminded her, "Now you got some money. Somebody just handed you a check for ten grand. You can leave it with your family and take your trip on up to the pearly gates."

"Nope," Harriet said, "I am going to die, probably later tonight. I have already talked to God about it. Feeling guilty about not giving those hungry lions my money was silly. They will have to find someone else's bones to fight over. I only have one thing left to do before I can go to Heaven."

"What's that, ma'm?" George asked.

"I've got to give somebody this check," Harriet smiled. "Didn't you wonder why I asked you to hear my story?"

"No, ma'm," the maintenance man answered, "Just because I happened to be in here?"

"Of course not, George. I know your wife has been sick. You need some help with her bills. Take this check before you go and do not tell anybody. If you snitch on me, I'll take back every cent. I won't take no for an answer"

With that, she pressed the already endorsed check into the man's hands and shooed him out the open door.

Later that night, old Aunt Harriet went to be with the LORD. She was smiling and appeared quite peaceful, according to her hospice nurse.

EDUARDO

Eduardo made a good living for himself, his wife Angelica and their two young boys. Jorge was four years old and already quite precocious. Eduardo, Jr. was laid-back and aware of others, an unusual trait for a two-year old. All four loved their family life. Happiness was evident.

Eduardo was the gift shop manager at the fanciest hotel in a tourist island nation. His boss, "Mr. Skip" was considered the best professional manager in the city's hospitality industry. He had crafted a reputation for honesty and ability that extended far beyond the island. For some reason, "Skip" had taken an instant liking to Eduardo, a young man from the other side of the island. Promotion to managerial status came quickly for the young man. Much bigger things than gift shop manager could be in store for Eduardo. The future looked bright indeed.

Everyone in the capitol city knew about the rebel uprising out in the countryside. Most of the citizens went about their business as usual, as they prepared for the country's raucous New Year's Eve celebration. Many tourists were flying in for the festivities. Eduardo's hotel was especially busy, hosting a presidential party and celebration. Most of the top government officials, including the nation's president, would be attending. The coming new year looked promising, even with the civil unrest.

Then everything changed. During the party at the hotel, gunshots were heard in the street outside. Murmurs began circulating about the rebels entering the capitol city and seizing control of the government. Then the president himself took the stage and announced that he would be fleeing the island. Panic ensued as partygoers began running from the hotel. Eduardo watched everything unfold from his vantage point in the gift shop, located in the hotel lobby. Shortly after midnight, the bearded rebel leader appeared in person. He stopped at the gift shop and asked Eduardo the name of the hotel manager. When Eduardo had answered "Mr. Skip", the rebel chief ordered him to summon the manager immediately. "Mr. Skip" quickly appeared. After a terse greeting, the pistol toting rebel chief demanded all keys to the property. As "Mr. Skip" fished the keys from his suit pocket, he asked about collecting his own family and leaving the island for the U. S. mainland. The camouflage garbed rebel laughed and said "You can leave the hotel in the morning. We will allow you to spend the night here, but at a special rate of $300 for the room." Edwardo knew that the average rental rate for a standard room was $100. "Mr. Skip" just nodded, with a wry grin on his face. The celebration ended and the new year had barely begun.

Eduardo was allowed to continue as manager of the hotel gift shop. However, a seemingly innocent conversation several months later had landed him in trouble with the new rebel government. A national news magazine from the United States had a cover story on the bearded leader of the revolution. A tourist in the gift shop made a derogatory remark about the cover and the rebel's open affection for communism. The customer had asked for Eduardo's opinion. The young gift shop manager replied "Yes, he does seem to be enamored with communism." Unbeknownst to Eduardo, the man questioning him was a reporter for a major American newspaper.

The publication ran a long article the next day that quoted Eduardo by name. That very night, he received a knock on his casa door. Several rifle toting rebels arrested him on the spot. He was brought to a facility being used for interrogating dissidents. Many of those being questioned later disappeared without explanation.

The probes were mild at first. Eduardo assured his accusers that he barely remembered making the remark. He denied involvement with any group opposed to the rebel regime.

The gift shop manager was tossed into a cell overnight and the questioning continued the next morning. All gentleness disappeared. There were four rebel soldiers who took turns haranguing him. They demanded that Eduardo implicate anyone else that might be plotting against the new government. One of the interrogators yelled at him and slapped his ears several times. Another soldier leaned close into the young man's face and roared damning accusations. Then, the largest of the questioners physically picked him up and propelled his body against a wall. After a few more hours of mistreatment, Eduardo was manhandled outside of the building and tossed into the street. There were promises of stiffer punishment if his name ever surfaced again as someone opposed to the rebel government.

Eduardo drug himself home, covered in blood and bruises. His wife and two sons were terrified by his appearance. That night, they considered their options as a family. In a rare gesture, Eduardo implored his family to get down on their knees with him. "We need to ask God for deliverance," he said, "The Holy Father is our only hope." The next day, he reported for work as usual. As he opened the gift shop, Eduardo found a "customer" waiting for him. It was "Mr. Skip". He was in disguise, sporting a fake beard and wearing dark sunglasses. Eduardo recognized the former hotel manager and was quite surprised to see him back on the island.

"Mr. Skip" motioned for the young man to come closer. Then, he whispered: "Meet me outside at the back of the hotel in five minutes. Call Angelica and the boys. Let her know the family will be picked up in ten minutes in front of your house. Tell them not to bring any suitcases or personal items. This must be a quick getaway. Explain to them that that a white van will be waiting. It will take them to meet you at a private dock where a boat has been chartered. The boat will bring you to the U. S. That's it. I'll meet you in a couple of minutes. Just walk out of the gift shop naturally. There is a detail of rebel soldiers coming right now to arrest you. You should just barely miss them. Do not delay. Your life and your family's future depends on what happens in the next few minutes." With that, "Mr. Skip" was out the door and gone.

Everything went as planned. The 90-mile trip across the water went smoothly and without incident. A welcoming party of exiles in the Florida Keys then assumed control. They furnished Eduardo and his family with new identities and comfortable living quarters. It did not take long for the new immigrant to establish himself as a respected businessman in the community. The family prospered. Both Jorge and Eduardo, Jr. graduated from college. Jorge went on to medical school, while Junior became a successful attorney and popular politician. The day that Eduardo, Jr. was sworn into the state legislature as a newly elected senator, Eduardo and Angelica were in the gallery. They proudly watched as their son took the oath of office. As Eduardo surveyed the crowd at the ceremony, he spotted a familiar face. The man was much older now and appeared somewhat frail. But it was clearly "Mr. Skip". Eduardo quickly leaped from his seat, pulling Angelica with him as he sped over to greet his old friend and savior. He swooped down on the old man and grasped his hand tightly.

"Mr. Skip", he cried, "How can I ever thank you for what you did for me and my family. You rescued us from the lions' den. We owe you so much. God bless you, sir."

"Thank you, Eduardo," the surprised old man said, looking up in confusion. "But I have no idea what you are talking about."

GOD AND DANIEL HANG OUT A LOT TOGETHER

Of course, God loves everybody. After all, Spirit created each soul with care and precision. It does not matter the color, creed, gender or geographical location involved. Our omnipresent, omnipotent and omniscient God gave birth to one and all.

But now the truth can be revealed. God does have Its special favorites.

The Old Testament prophet Daniel ranks at the very top of The Creator's Hall of Fame. The pair meet regularly to review current events and future trends. God values Daniel's insights and opinions. The Creator seeks the prophet's views on both world and heavenly issues. After all, Daniel ranks as one of the premier dreams and visions interpreters in the entire Bible. As such, God likes to hear his thoughts on various happenings and trends. Some of their conversations have already changed human and spiritual history. God and Daniel's most recent talk offers an example of their heavenly dialogue:

GOD: "So what do you think about your planet right now?"

DANIEL: "Could you be more specific, LORD? Do you mean physically, morally, mentally, or spiritually?"

GOD: "How about a short take on each one?"

DANIEL: "Physically, the world eco-systems are reeling for many reasons. Climate change is just the most obvious. Humankind has not been the best steward. But there are some dedicated people trying to change things. I am still hopeful, that is if the nuclear weapons stay under lock and key. Of course, everything could also change if one those pesky asteroids goes off course again. Is somebody up here on top of that? Or did you give free will to the Milky Way too?"

GOD: "No comment. Let's stay respectful. Where do you see human morals headed?"

DANIEL: "Are you kidding? That's the black hole for the world. I thought it was bad in my day. Every single one my four kings was amoral, to say the least. King Neb was the worst. Almost every night was a drunken orgy. He operated on the Jimmy Buffet premise."

GOD: "What's that?"

DANIEL: "It is always five o'clock somewhere."

GOD: "What else is bothering you about the moral climate?"

DANIEL: "I am concerned about almost everything! Children learn to swear before they can recite their ABCs. Gambling is everywhere. The school boards will be putting slot machines in the elementary grade bathrooms before it ends. And, dear LORD, please do not get me started about pornography. The nursing homes are the hot spots now, pardon the pun. Major scandals among the elderly are in the works as we speak. And, lastly, let us not turn a blind eye to our old friend "politics". Today's money is far too attractive for those so-called "lawmakers". I am sure you remember that Evil's biggest world embassy is right there on "K" Street. You knew that already, right? We've been raving about politics up here since back in my day. Money, sex and power are still the biggest corrupters. There are so many lost souls now. The earth is in a sad moral state. You need to instruct Moses to re-issue the 10 Commandments. Maybe he should add a couple of extra tablets on gambling and pornography."

GOD: "How well I know the problems. In fact, that is one reason that I wanted to see you. I have been thinking about how you interpreted those dreams and visions back in the day. You explained the meaning of "the handwriting on the wall." I think the "handwriting" is out there again. Now, if only the world leaders will pay attention. Time is running out. The forces of evil are capturing souls left and right. It is only a matter of time before something catastrophic happens. I will not allow evil to triumph forever. I think that you may need to go back and do more dream and vision interpreting for the world's big shots. Something needs to happen and soon. How would you feel about a special assignment? I know you are settled and happy here, but your skills are needed elsewhere for a while."

DANIEL: "Of course, My LORD, just let me know. It would be my greatest honor to serve the Kingdom of Heaven again. Send me. I will gladly go. I agree the world is teetering right now."

GOD: "I knew you would respond that way, Dan. I have a list of future dreams and visions right here in front of Me. Your incarnation begins tonight. It will be a full schedule for a while. My beloved children are struggling. Some of their top leaders need a wake-up call. These dreams will frighten them, as they did with your various kings. I guarantee you today's rulers will be looking for somebody to interpret them. That is where you can come in again. Thank you for taking on this assignment. I AM grateful, as usual."

DANIEL: "It is my greatest pleasure, Father. Let's go to work."

MY OWN LIONS' DEN STORY

Here is the situation:

Why it feels like a lions' den.

What are my options?

This is what I would ask of God:

Thank you God. (Signed)

A FINAL THOUGHT
HOW OUR ENEMIES BLESS US

You might be walking into a den of lions today. You may be traveling along life's road with no rough patches, potholes, detours or distractions. Suddenly, you hear some threatening roars. Before you can react, ferocious and hungry lions surround you. You are their prey. They look ready to tear you apart. What can you do? Maybe only a few seconds remain before the they attack and devour you. Remember, it could happen today.

Anytime you find yourself a perilous situation, never hesitate. Call out for God's divine intervention. Ask for deliverance from the dark and dangerous places where life has taken you. Seek divine guidance without delay. Discuss your best options with God. You can pound on Heaven's door day or night, seeking wisdom and protection. Your Higher Power waits for just such a moment. God wants to help rescue you from the roaring lions. There is no danger or situation that our Creator cannot overcome. Never give yourself up to any den of lions, no matter how threatening they seem. The LORD offers hope for the hopeless, courage for the frightened and comfort for the afflicted. Stand tall.

Face the approaching lions with confidence. You have nothing to fear.

Also be aware of how our enemies can bless us. Their desire may be to bring trouble or even destroy us. But the story of Daniel in the Lions' Den illustrates how opposing forces can be a blessing. Because Daniel kept his faith in God, he was delivered from all harm. His steadfastness earned him greater credibility with the kings that he served. Without the roaring lions and the prospect of imminent death, Daniel would not have been able to demonstrate God's Power. This same principle can be true in our own lives. When we show how trusting God helped us overcome life's greatest challenges, we build credibility with everyone in our sphere of influence. The enemies around us may have meant their destructiveness for harm. But, by maintaining our faith in God, we can produce a blessing of Good instead. Without those enemies who attack and threaten us, we would have no way to demonstrate God's miracles of power and deliverance.

THE END

ABOUT THE AUTHOR

Rev. Allen C. Liles is a graduate of Baylor University in Waco, TX and The Unity School of Religious Studies at Unity Village, MO. Before being ordained as a non-denominational minister in 1993, he served as the vice-president for public relations at The Southland Corporation (7-Eleven Stores) in Dallas, TX. and Communications Manager for The McLane Company in Temple, TX. Rev. Liles was also Senior Director of Outreach for the Unity School of Christianity from 1995-2001 and senior minister for Unity Churches in Missouri, Arizona and Minnesota. He is the originator and author of the new "Classic Bible Chapters" series.

BOOKS BY ALLEN C. LILES

Exodus 20: The Ten Commandants

Ephesians 6: Putting On the Full Armor of God

John 14: The Most Important Chapter in the New Testament

Sitting With God: Meditating for God's Divine Guidance

The 7 Puzzles of Life: God's Plan to Save the World

The Forever Penny: How Our Loved Ones Stay Connected After Death

Oh Thank Heaven: The Story of the Southland Corporation

E-Books on www.smashwords.com

The 12 Promises of Heaven

Friends of Jesus

www.ingramcontent.com/pod-product-compliance
Lightning Source LLC
LaVergne TN
LVHW010105110826
845155LV00028B/489

* 9 7 8 1 9 5 1 7 7 6 6 3 3 *